How to Properly Relate in the Ministry of Giving

Phylisa Dever

Dedication

I dedicate this book to my Heavenly Father, who has inspired me to share my experience. I look forward to growing in Him. In Him, I live, move, and have my being. It is because of Him that we are where we are in life. He's our source for everything.

I dedicate this book to my loving mother, Levada Blair, who has always believed and supported me in everything that I have touched. Being your daughter has been a great privilege. You are the most unselfish and generous person that I know. You taught me that I could be or do anything that I desired in life. I love you, Mama.

To my husband, Joseph Dever Jr., you are truly a gift from God to not only me but my family. I met you 22 years ago, and we have been married for 21 years. The last 21 years of my life have been some of the most awesome years of my life. You have taught me so much, and we have grown by leaps and bounds. I am so thankful to have you in my life. You are truly a living example of Jesus in the earth realm. You have done everything in your power to help me and the children fulfill our dreams. You're not selfish. You're like my mother, generous and loving. May we all grow closer and closer to our Heavenly Father.

Acknowledgment

I would like to thank each and every individual for supporting me in this effort. I am very thankful to have people like you in my life. Again I say thank you from the bottom of my heart for believing in me and supporting me in this effort with your love and support. There are others that I didn't name, and I say thank you to everyone.

Joseph L. Dever Jr., Orlando, Florida

Shawnice Hurt, Orlando, Florida

Levada Blair, Orlando, Florida

Walter Sonny Hill, Wildwood Florida

Suzanne Johnson, Steyer Maryland

Cynthia Roberts, Orlando, Florida

Linda Blair, Phenix City, Alabama

Melinda King, Phenix City, Alabama

Tracey Adams, Augusta, Georgia

Joe Blair Jr., Ashburn, Virginia

Rashad Taylor, Miami, Florida

Sandy McHardy, Titusville, Florida

John Robinson, Orlando, Florida

Kirk Martinez, Orlando, Florida

San Janette Scott, Orlando, Florida

Nancy Rulong, Orlando, Florida

Freda Johnson, Houston, Texas

Eric Johnson, Orlando, Florida

Christabel Mcintosh, Orlando, Florida

Betty Runyon, Orlando, Florida

Jan Bocash, Orlando, Florida

Jewell Johnson, Orlando, Florida

Page Left Blank Intentionally

Contents

Introduction

The purpose behind my book is to inform and share with you about an important ministry that has changed my life, which encourages action and lifestyle that brings glory to God, The Ministry of Giving.

I was prompted by two main reasons to write this book. One was to inform you how to properly relate to the Ministry of giving. Having lived through a life-changing experience spanning across two decades, not merely me, but my whole family is much better off than where we started. I desired that my readers also learn how to properly relate to the Ministry of giving so that they may flourish too.

The second reason for writing this book was to caution you against manipulators. I hoped that by reading this book, you develop the understanding of steering clear of predators who are after your money. You may find them in your friends, relatives, or in your church Preachers like I had. They manipulate you in the name of giving, coercing you to do things you don't want to do.

I have written this book from the bottom of my heart. All the ideas I talk about here with the purpose of making you relate to the Ministry of Giving; I have learned them with time.

The knowledge about the principles of giving came to me the hard way. It took me to go through some unpleasant experiences. I've learned valuable lessons that turned out to be blessings.

Amongst other things, this book is inspired by an experience that my husband and I went through. We are a Christian family that was a part of a Church community for twenty-one years, and we lived by the Ministry of Giving. It is in this Ministry that we raised our family. Our children grew up learning these very principles.

Chapter 1
The Background

In the year 2000, my husband and I went to a conference. The guest speaker there, Prophetess Cynthia P. Roberts, grabbed my hand and told my Pastor that my husband and I are called to the Ministry of Giving. This was the first time that I had ever heard of such a thing. I was as curious as you might be about this right now.

When the Holy Bible says, *"Whether therefore you eat, or drink, or whatsoever ye do, do all to the glory of God" (1 Corinthians 10:31 KJV),* we know that a Christian is one whose every act in life is spent doing deeds that bring glory to our Lord and Father in Heaven.

Throughout its pages, the Bible asks us to live a life of generosity. In Exodus chapter 35, the people of Israel not only give of their resources but also their time to build the tabernacle. When our Father asks us of generosity, he is, in a way, asking us to imitate him. God gave us this life, this world with its countless blessings, our family and loved ones, and most importantly, His only son so that we might be saved, though he knew Christ would die on the cross. God himself is the leader of the Ministry of giving, and as faithful servants, he leads us into that Ministry.

When I refer to the act of giving as Ministry, what I am saying is that it is a continuous function. Being generous is not a seasonal act; it is a perpetual action that carries on for life; it is a lifestyle, a way of being. The Bible calls it a ministry, and says the following:

"10 Now he that ministereth seed to the sower both minister bread for your food, and multiply your seed sown, and increase the fruits of your righteousness;)

11 Being enriched in everything to all bountifulness, which causeth through us thanksgiving to God.

12 For the administration of this service not only supplieth the want of the saints but is abundant also by many thanksgivings unto God;

13 Whiles by the experiment of this ministration they glorify God for your professed subjection unto the Gospel of Christ, and for your liberal distribution unto them, and unto all men." (*2 Corinthians 9:10-13 KJV*)

The message goes that two things will result from us abiding by the Ministry of giving in our lives: we shall supply to the needs of the people and glorify God with our gratitude towards Him.

Generosity is special, for it is through the act of giving that we identify and recognize what love is. If you think about Christmas, what makes it special is the idea of giving. We spread joy and generosity all around during the Christmas season when we give and receive. These actions happen out of love. I don't need to tell you how much each of us craves love. Giving in one form or another is the perfect expression of that love.

When I think about giving, I am so filled with love for God. As opposed to the concept of giving that we perceive it, that is, taking something out of your possession and passing it on to the other. The act of giving is *an act of getting*. That is just how God has organized the world. The Bible says:

"There is one who scatters yet increases more; And there is one who withholds more than is right, but it leads to poverty." (**Proverbs 11:24 NKJV**)

When we give from our resources, our resources expand. When we give, it may appear as if we're subtracting from what we have, but in the long run, it becomes an act of multiplication. *Hebrews 13:16* **NIV** calls for doing good and sharing with others an act of "sacrifice" that pleases God. His blessings attract the generous hand and put more into that hand. After all, God is the greatest of all givers. He gives to the people even when they withhold.

The concept of withholding has been mentioned in the Bible to contrast the idea of giving. Hoarding and withholding are selfish acts. These things only bring the illusion of having something. It brings damage to the soul, which thrives on the happiness of others and helping them. That is the idea given in the Proverbs verse above. In truth, not only are we blessed in this world when we give, but our treasures increase in Heaven as well. The Bible says:

"Do not store up for yourselves treasures on earth, where moths and vermin destroy, and where thieves break in and steal. But store up for yourselves [by giving] treasures in Heaven, where moths and vermin do not destroy, and where thieves do not break in and steal. For where your treasure is, there your heart will be also." **(*Matthew 6:19-21 NIV*)**

My mother also joined the Church within the first year, and eventually, so did my sister and her children. Our family, all together, along with our grandbabies, make a total of fifteen of us who were members of this congregation. As you will read on, I hope that I inspire you to participate in the Ministry of giving too. In this book, you will learn how to properly relate to the Ministry of giving.

This is something that we operate in. I have worked on this principle for over twenty years, and I am astonished by how my life has changed! I have seen God take us from having nothing to having more than enough to bless and help others. We know what it's like to have nothing, so there is more heart in our giving than reluctance or any feeling of pressure. We have given millions of dollars to the Kingdom of God, and this giving has become a part of my identity. I am proud to say this is who I am. Jesus said, *"I became poor that you may be rich" (2 Corinthians 8:9 KJV)*. I live by this principle too. I know that God is my source. On my own, I am nothing. I cannot say that it is I who gives, for what power do I have over myself? If it hadn't been for the heart that God gave me, and the experiences that he acquainted me with, I would not be this person. It's not because of my strength or my will that I have, but because of my Lord Jesus Christ. He has made us the Distribution Center for the Kingdom of God, and I cannot be happier. I love Jesus with all of my heart, soul, and being.

My faith and dependence upon God are not unjustified. In **Deuteronomy 8:18 NIV** the Bible tells us, *"But remember the Lord your God, for it is he who gives you the ability to produce wealth, and so confirms his covenant, which he swore to your ancestors, as it is today."* Not only my wealth, but my very ability to produce wealth comes from God. The same principles that led my ancestors to success in this world apply to me, which is why I live in the Ministry of giving.

God is all about abundance. Hence he is sure to love abundance. In **John 10:10 KJV**, he says, *"The thief cometh not, but for to steal, and to kill, and to destroy: I am come that they might have life and that they might have it more abundantly."* God contrasts himself to a thief reversing the roles and functions of the two. The thief steals out of your possessions for selfish means. Meanwhile, God grants all that mankind receives. Life in abundance means having Salvation first, health, and then wealth so that you can be a blessing to whomever the Lord directs you to.

On earth, we need money to take care of business in life. ***Ecclesiastes 10:19 KJV*** says that money *"answereth all things,"* while food encourages laughter and wine is about merriment. The question is, what is the money the answer to? It is the answer to all the needs. Whatever we want to obtain in life, money supplies it.

The meals and wine that the verse talks about are bought using money. But there is a transcendent quality to money as well. It is in its sharing and giving that we come to witness that quality. While the consumption of money makes the body and heart prosper, the distribution of money makes the soul prosper. Now, the act of giving is not merely about taking from your possession and handing money to another. God wants us to give with character, rather than offering mindlessly.

The Bible says, *"Or he that exhorteth, on exhortation:* ***he that giveth, let him do it with simplicity;*** *he that ruleth, with diligence; he that showeth mercy, with cheerfulness."*

I have had experiences with people who have not been virtuous nor principled givers. They did a lot of things that were not righteous in the area of giving. Pressure was put on us, and we were forced to contribute money, which never felt good. My husband and I felt guilty about not giving and criticize the amount we would contribute.

We were asked to do something that the Bible warns us against, which is to co-sign for a building for them. Even though the Pastor had taught us scriptures against co-signing for anyone, they turned on those beliefs and asked not only us but others as well. The first time, my husband and I refused to do so, for we knew it was wrong.

When asked again, my husband felt bad, and their manipulation worked. They got my husband to co-sign, and we later learned that they did not pay the rent on the building. Now we are in a situation where not only we were manipulated, but we are now in a bad spot. My job as a Minister of Jesus Christ is to inform and empower you, the reader, and others to listen to the voice of the Holy Spirit in the acts you do to glorify God. Make sure it is a faith move as well as a God move when helping others. When something does not align with your spirit, it is ok to decline the offer. I hope that by reading this book, you get the awareness about how you should not fall prey to manipulations in the name of giving. Be it a Pastor, your own friend, just make sure they are not making you do something you do not feel comfortable doing.

If you give, give from a place of purity in your heart; otherwise, you will not be able to reap full reward. People deserve to be empowered, who are vigilant believers and not without faith. Find the moderation between giving and knowing when and whom to give. Do not make the same mistakes that we did.

Let me bring your attention to *Ephesians 4: 12-14*. The Bible says, *12 "For the perfecting of the saints, for the work of the ministry, for the edifying of the body of Christ:"*

That verse means that the purpose of various ministries, of which giving is one in which the saints are perfected with their spiritual growth and conjoin to make one body of Jesus Christ. Then the Bible says:

13 "Till we all come into the unity of the faith, and of the knowledge of the Son of God, unto a perfect man, unto the measure of the stature of the fullness of Christ."

14 "That we henceforth be no more children, tossed to and fro, and carried about with every wind of doctrine, by the sleight of men, and cunning craftiness, whereby they lie, in wait to deceive."

Chapter 2
Philanthropy

*"If among you, one of your brothers should become poor,
in any of your towns within your land that the Lord your
God is giving you, you shall not harden your heart or shut
your hand against your poor brother, but you shall open
your hand to him and lend him sufficient for his need,
whatever it may be."*

-Deuteronomy 15:7

At some point in your life, you may have wanted to be rich someday, so you could donate to humanitarian causes. You may have wanted to start charities that share compassion and prosperity with the community.

Without knowing it, you wanted to become a philanthropist. The practice of philanthropy is led by the desire to promote the welfare of others. The desire is expressed by the generous donation of money to a good cause as a charity. A philanthropist then is a person who gives money or gifts to charities or helps people in other ways. The Bible has taught us the virtues of philanthropy. Someone who gives from a cheerful hand realizes that giving in the Bible is a practice of faith, obedience, and, most importantly, love. Your freely giving hand, and one that shares with others openly, unconditionally, and free from selfishness, reflects what your heart is like. Most importantly, you are reminded not only that you merely profess your love for God and Christ but that you show it in tangible ways as well.

In this chapter, I will speak about the different categories within philanthropy in the Bible. These include Tithing, Offerings, Building Fund, Missions, Missionaries, and Evangelism. We will then learn of the examples of the biblical figures you and I should look up to as role model philanthropists. Then, we will briefly look at how some scientific facts back up generosity and ultimately look at the big names in the world of philanthropy today.

Tithing

The word "tithe" is commonly misused and misperceived today. It is used in relation to any church-related giving. The word tithe originally means "tenth."

The obligatory offering in the Law of Moses commanded 10% of Israelite's first. The harvest was a blessing from God, so the earliest reaping was given back to them. That was the central idea around the term. God reminded the Israelites that the things they have are not, in fact, theirs. They were His. As an exercise of thankfulness, they were asked to provide tithes for the Levitical priesthood, festivals.

Offering

Offerings are considered to be gifts, given outside of or in addition to the tithe.

While the Mosaic Law requires tithing as an obligation, an offering is not a compulsion upon the believer. It is a voluntary 'offering,' quite literally, of some form of a donation to a church or charity. Outside of money, an offering can be volunteered to any community service to carry out God's work helping mankind. Back in the biblical time, people made sacrifices as an offering to God in addition to giving. Compared to that, our offerings symbolize an act of worship.

During the worship service, the offering becomes an opportunity for us believers to become the recipients of grace, love, and mercy of God. By making an offering, we put the faith and trust deep down within us for the Lord into tangible action.

Building Fund

11 When the amount had been determined, they gave the money to the men appointed to supervise the work on the temple. With it, they paid those who worked on the temple of the LORD – the carpenters and builders,

12 The masons and stonecutters. They purchased timber and blocks of dressed stone for the repair of the temple of the LORD and met all the other expenses of restoring the temple.

13 The money brought into the temple was not spent for making silver basins, wick trimmers, sprinkling bowls, trumpets or any other articles of gold or silver for the temple of the LORD;

*14 it was paid to the workers, who used it to repair the temple. **2 Kings 12:11-14 NIV***

The verses above are some of the many examples given in the Bible, where the people were commanded to give for the construction of a church or temple. The maintenance of the holy place, its worship, and the Ministry required this funding. We, as Christians, are aware that each of our churches set up fundraising initiatives for new projects. It could be a fellowship hall or a sanctuary, the contribution to which is considered highly significant. Other times, churches reserve the money or raise it for the sake of reparations pertaining to existing buildings rather than expanding the premises or starting something new.

You may be giving to individuals or the Church in person, but spiritually, you are giving to God. This form of giving establishes and sets in stone your personal faith in the Son of God. This is why you should donate an amount to the people of God and the work they do. Be careful about who you are giving to. It is essential, and well within your rights, to verify that your money will be put to good use.

Missions

The Bible tells us that the final command Jesus gave to his disciples was nothing but to

"19 Go ye therefore, and teach all nations, baptizing them in the name of the Father, and of the Son, and of the Holy Ghost:

*20 Teaching them to observe all things whatsoever I have commanded you: and, lo, I am with you always, even unto the end of the world. Amen." (**Matthew 28:19-20 KJV**).*

As Christians who believe in Christ and the salvation bound to him, it is our duty to spread the word of God across the world.

By carrying out missions, we are doing a service to God. Preaching the divine message to the unbelievers has been at the core of Christian values and worship. They are in need of God's mercy, which they receive in the form of missionaries who bring them the Gospel. It makes Him work in the depths of their hearts.

What we sometimes do not realize is that missions are not a vanity project, nor is it a lowly function of the Ministry. It is sometimes mistreated that way, which breaks my heart. Missions are the crown jewel atop the head of Christian worship. David exalts in it, for which Christ commands, and Paul the Apostle ceaselessly labors for it.

*"For you remember, brothers, our labor and toil: we worked night and day, that we might not be a burden to any of you, while we proclaimed to you the gospel of God." (**1 Thessalonians 2:9 ESV**).*

Missionaries

Missionaries are included amongst the list of prestigious givers. They do not only give out of their pockets but directly out of their hearts. This form of wealth is as tangible as any currency of the world.

There certainly are many missionaries mentioned in the Bible who did God's good work by carrying out the missions. Undoubtedly, Jesus Christ is the most prestigious among them. The Son of God abandoned His home for our sake in Heaven and traveled the land (Earth), making it from his spiritual to earthly form. He was the living Gospel who brought the message of God through his very life.

Evangelism

Evangelism and Missions are similar, but they are not the same. Missions focus on the idea of sending a believer off, usually through divine inspiration, to disperse the Gospel. Evangelism relates to the act of publicly preaching the Gospel without being sent off, particularly by divine command. As long as you have the intention of spreading the Gospel and what Jesus taught, you are fulfilling the role of an evangelist. Evangelists can be within their homes, communities, or living as missionaries in the field. The theme of evangelism frequently appears in the Bible. One of the scriptures says:

"But in your hearts revere Christ as Lord. Always be prepared to give an answer to everyone who asks you to give the reason for the hope that you have. But do this with gentleness and respect..." **(1 Peter 3:15 NIV)**

We learned about the various forms of giving above. They are associated across various ministries. You might not be able to give to every Ministry, and that is not an obligation. However, you give, for whichever of these Ministries, none other than the Holy Spirit should be your guide in the giving. The Bible says those that are led by the Spirit of God are the Sons of God. We may never reach the rank and stature Jesus has, but it is an honor for us to stand behind him in the ranks by winning the lost by giving.

Examples of Giving from Biblical Figures
Abraham

God was going to show a new land to Abraham and give it to him and his descendants. It was a major event, a big blessing for Abraham. But he did not enjoy it alone.

Abraham allowed his nephew Lot and Lot's people to come along with him and his wife. Together, he invited them to visit the new land gifted by God. Nothing shows your generous spirit more than inviting your family to share your joy and merriment, especially when the giver is God. People usually want to gather the pleasantries by themselves, but not Abraham.

Abraham was not only a generous giver, but a principled one, and very wise too. He refused the loot given to him upon rescuing Lot and the captives of war, resulting in the spike of troubled. Only a very wise giver like Abraham can refuse treasures from the people already troubled, though he may be deserving of it.

The final example of Abraham's generosity was, of course, his hospitality. He was known for hosting people and visitors passing by. He would even go out in search sometimes and give people shade from the scorching heat and a fulfilling meal.

Noah

Noah is well known in the Bible for the great flood mentioned in the old testament book of Genesis. The God of

Israel, in whom nature's capacity to protect from a world-consuming disastrous catastrophe is secured, holds Noah as the ideal of a righteous man.

Having received the divine assignment by the Lord to build the ark for a flood that was going to wipe away everything on land. The flood was the resultant of the corruption that God beheld on the earth. As His wrath, God became determined to annihilate it.

He instructed Noah to bring a male and a female pair of all the species of the animal kingdom on earth into the ark. There was an exception for people, among whom all were invited upon the ark.

This event marked the apex of generosity. Noah, having built the ark, extended his kindness and favor towards not just people, but the animals.

Solomon

King Solomon's might was far-reaching in his life alone. He reigned on earth. He is known for his generosity and the caretaking he subjected to his nation.

When another mighty ruler, Queen Sheba, heard about him, she gifted him around 120 tablets of gold and stocky amounts of Balsam and other medicinal oils and precious stones. If the price of that gold was converted to today's dollar, the amount would be equal to $40,000,000. At the time, the oils she offered to King Solomon was considered with gold as a valuable commodity. In *1 Kings 10:*101NIV, the Bible tells us that her gift remained incomparable to any other offering granted before.

In response, the Bible says, *"King Solomon gave the queen of Sheba all she desired and asked for; he gave her more than she had brought to him. Then she left and returned with her retinue to her own country."* (*2 Chronicles 9:12 NIV*)

And king Solomon gave unto the queen of Sheba all her desire, whatsoever she asked, beside that which Solomon gave her of his royal bounty. So she turned and went to her own country, she and her servants. (*1 Kings 10:13 KJV*)

While gift-exchanging was a custom even back then, the Bible specifically mentions Solomon's *"openhandedness"* (*1 Kings 10:13 ESV*) in all matters and in all his giving. Solomon himself is known to have said:

"The liberal soul shall be made fat: and he that watereth shall be watered also himself." **(Proverbs 11:25 KJV)**

These are people that actually worked the biblical principles and reaped a harvest. They worked and got results.

Science and Giving

By this point, we know that God loves the charitable.

"Through Him then let us continually offer up a sacrifice of praise to God, that is, the fruit of lips that acknowledge his name. Do not neglect to do good and to share what you have, for such sacrifices are pleasing to God." **(Hebrews 13:15-16 ESV)**

In His eyes, one who gives out of himself and for the favor of another reaps a harvest. Any other person who shows off exhibits a lack of faith in God and His Son. God gives back in bounties to the openhanded soul.

But these are all benefits from the religious side. Let us hear what science has to say about generosity.

According to research, donors and volunteers who serve a cause for the benefit of others tend to live 20% longer than non-donors. People with high participation in charitable events have also been known to have lower cholesterol, blood pressure, and lower BMI's. Doing charity also has emotional advantages like the happiness that comes from watching a smile on a person's face when you do something for them. Charity and fundraising events have a lot of social involvement, which benefits with networking.

These benefits have been known to be experienced by some of the wealthiest philanthropists in the world in today's time. Let us consider my favorite three among them.

John D. Rockefeller

John D. Rockefeller was the founder of Standard Oil Company. He became one of the world's wealthiest men and a major philanthropist. He is my favorite because he was a man who loved God. He was a Baptist, and he acknowledged that God was the reason behind his success. Rockefeller donated more than half a billion dollars to various educational, religious, and scientific causes through his foundation. He funded the establishment of the University of Chicago and the Rockefeller Institute of Medical Research, now Called the Rockefeller University.

Warren Buffet

Warren Buffet also donates to a non-profit organization that he runs in the name of his late first wife. Two other non-profits go by his three children's names.

Buffet's 2019 donations totaled up to $3.6 billion, making his total donations since 2006 as $34 billion. In 2006, Warren Buffett had pledged to give $37 billion in stock to the Bill and Melinda Gates Foundation to be used for health and education purposes. He has been making progress year by year to complete that promised amount.

Oprah Winfrey

Who can forget about Oprah Winfrey? Her name always comes to mind when talking about being benevolent and giving.

This one of America's greatest talk show host has donated millions of dollars to about 31 charities and organizations that have spanned to 27 different causes. With that being said, most of Oprah's money goes to three foundations: The Angel Network, The Oprah Winfrey Foundation, and The Oprah Winfrey Operating Foundation.

The wealthy and the righteous understand that with wealth comes responsibility. Whether they know it or not, they are working a Biblical principle. Amassing wealth does not satisfy anyone. The secret to living is giving, and so is the secret to happiness. By giving, you purify your wealth, satisfy the Father in Heavens, and reinforce your belief in Jesus Christ. This principle is stated throughout the Bible.

Chapter 3
Stumbling Blocks

Acquiring a generous, giving personality is a process. You are, going from selfishness, a state of openhandedness; this is a characteristic of selfless people. As it is with all journeys, you will encounter stumbling blocks on your path to building a generous character.

There are six of the most common stumbling blocks we faced on our road to generosity, and more generally, towards success. These stumbling blocks include:

- Pride,
- Poor Planning,
- Not Saving Money,
- Counting Other's Money,
- Working with the Wrong People,
- Not Learning from Your Mistakes.

I have been around people who possessed all six of these.

Stumbling Block #1: Pride

Pride is a problem for humanity. Pride's been defined as a feeling of deep pleasure or satisfaction in an achievement, accomplishment, or in someone else or something else. However, it's also been described as conceit, egotism, vanity, vainglory, all over one's own appearance or status in life and not just something that's been accomplished.

It is an inwardly directed emotion that can easily offend others and carries with it a connotation that displays an inflated sense of one's own worth or personal status and typically makes one feel a sense of superiority over others and can easily make someone look condescendingly at others.

Pride in one's nation or in one's own children is somewhat different from that of having pride in themselves (*Prov 17:6 KJV*), but even that can self-attribute a sense of worth that is easily overvalued, overinflated, and be unrealistic.

With pride comes a feeling of self-importance. Whether it is our thoughts or appearance, characteristics, or achievements that we become proud of. A rise in one's self-importance can only lead to one thing: depreciating the value and importance of others.

We either stay in competition with others or grow judgmental towards them. This builds self-centeredness that enviously and impatiently makes others appear beneath us.

It is suggested in the Bible (*Ezekiel 28:12-19 NIV*) that Satan was once a good angel who let his pride corrupt him, and thus, he fell (*"Like lightning from the heaven"* (*Luke 10:18 NIV*)). The offer he made to Adam and Eve in the Garden of Eden was nothing but an exercise of his pride. He challenged God by making the people disobey God, making them fall from grace. In one scripture, God gives Satan an interesting title.

"He is king over all the children of pride." (*Job 41:34 KJV*)

Thus, we have observed that pride belongs to the devil, and the devil is the adversary of God. Just as Satan intends to corrupt the righteous, so does pride. It steals all the room for love, and in the absence of love, there can be no meaningful generosity.

"[God] mocks proud mockers but shows favor to the humble and oppressed." (*Proverbs 3:34 NIV*)

The answer to pride, as ordained by God, is humbleness. To think lowly of oneself and realize that everyone is deserving of love and grace, including you, is the mindset to adopt. Once you get there, you will realize that the real pleasure comes through contributing to the benefit of others, which ultimately is what makes you happy.

I have encountered proud people in my life too. They would become a hindrance in our life, as well as in their own life without realizing it. There was a time earlier when my husband and a group of men approached the former Pastor about a poor business decision that would cost him the Church, but he would not listen. He would shoot everyone down because he was too stubborn to sway from his decision. There were many people that tried to help, but he would not budge from his decision. Due to his pride, we lost our investment because of his pride, which was the new Church facility.

Stumbling Block #2: Never Planning Properly

There are numerous virtues attached to the process of planning something properly. It entails wisdom, patience, insight, and farsightedness. All of that can be destroyed by a lack of planning, which. The Bible says:

"Wise people think before they act; fools don't – and even brag about their foolishness." **(Proverbs 13:16 NLT)**

We cannot build a house without sketching a plan first and modeling the structure. By doing so, we not only acquire a deeper understanding and knowledge of what we are producing but also eliminate risks of building a flawed structure and wasting resources. A foolish person goes with impulse and encounters all the dangers mentioned above. On this, the Bible says:

28 "Suppose one of you wants to build a tower. Won't you first sit down and estimate the cost to see if you have enough money to complete it?

29 For if you lay the foundation and are not able to finish it, everyone who sees it will ridicule you,

30 saying, 'This person began to build and wasn't able to finish." **(Luke 14:28-30 NIV)**

You cannot construct a home without blueprints just as you cannot begin new projects without planning them first.

Those who do not plan things properly have to pay

penalties – and they usually are in monetary form. Lack of proper timing and resource management costs them what good planning would have saved. Those who do not plan argue that planning takes time. The truth is it saves a lot of time and effort. It also saves your feelings of guilt and shame.

This is the benefit of reserving the time and efforts to plan. Make it part of your lifestyle as it is an ingredient to a philanthropic and successful life. It goes without saying that after making the plan, you have to stick to it as well. Otherwise, you are back to square one.

Stumbling Block #3: Never Saving Money

Not saving money is closely tied to the idea of planning ahead. The Bible has, at many places, condemned the spendthrift because they act in foolish ways and did not consider the rainy days that may come ahead. Saving money for family bills to come (education, mortgage, etc.) are indicators of a wise person who understands the importance of saving.

The Bible says:

"A slack hand causes poverty, but the hand of the diligent makes rich. He who gathers in summer is a prudent son, but he who sleeps in harvest is a son who brings shame." **(Proverbs 10:4-5 ESV)**

The Bible, in the same chapter, also says this:

"A good man leaves an inheritance to his children's children, but the sinner's wealth is laid up for the righteous." **(Proverbs 13:22 ESV)**

The act of saving money then becomes akin to virtue. And why should it not? It entails making sacrifices for not spending money in unnecessary ways so that the necessary costs for the future could be met easily.

I am reminded of the former Pastor again, who misused the preaching of saving money. He kept telling us that the month of October was the Clergy appreciation month. Everyone was supposed to save to make their goals of giving him an offering at the end of October. Coincidentally, his birthday also occurred around that time. He would emotionally blackmail us and become unhappy if we didn't make the goals. He never saved anything himself, that we knew for sure. I want to warn you about such people who may take advantage of you and your savings.

Stumbling Block #4: Counting on Other People's Money

Let us be honest. Nobody likes people who are concerned about other's wealth. These people invite repulsion, for they put their belief and faith in wealth. Neither the rich nor the poor are free from this vice.

"Command those who are rich in this present world not to be arrogant nor to put their hope in wealth, which is so uncertain, but to put their hope in God, who richly provides us with everything for our enjoyment." **(1 Timothy 6:17 NIV)**

In our experience, The Man of God was always counting our money. He would ask me questions about a lot of our finances. I ended up just telling him about contracts all of the time.

I remember one time my husband and I were supposed to get a $2.6 million contract. As soon as the former Pastor learned about it, he was counting on the tithes from that money to keep our building project going. Unfortunately for us, at least at that time, the company shopped around and chose another company. We didn't win the contract, and the old Pastor started to give my husband the cold shoulder and harsh treatment. He used to call him all the time, but after we lost the contract, he stopped calling. He was counting on our money. He confessed to my son and his girlfriend himself that the money my husband and I gave ran the Ministry. I noticed he did this with another couple also, and I just think it should not be like this. You are not responsible for others' expenses. Unless you are doing it out of your own happiness or by your will, people should not expect you to run their house or their projects for them. They should definitely not manipulate you in doing so.

We believe that he started to trust our hands and not trust God. He made us Idols, and God does not like Idols. He said that he is a Jealous God. Never trust the hand of man— trust God. He is your source.

The Bible has, condemned this attitude. It says:

"14 But if you have bitter jealousy and selfish ambition in your hearts, do not boast and be false to the truth.

15 This is not the wisdom that comes down from above but is earthly, unspiritual, demonic.

*16 For where jealousy and selfish ambition exist, there will be disorder and every vile practice." (**James 3:14-16 ESV**)*

I would further add that jealousy and selfish ambition are malicious ingredients that force you away from the things that matter. They stop you from helping the people you could help and keep you from looking after your own family. They keep you from being generous to your own self, let alone from others.

Stumbling Block #5: Choosing to Work with the Wrong People

*"Blessed is the man that walketh not in the counsel of the ungodly, nor standeth in the way of sinners, nor sitteth in the seat of the scornful." (**Psalm 1:1 KJV**)*

If you set off on a voyage on a ship, would you have a crew of efficient or incompetent sailors? Your choice is obvious. Likewise, whenever you decide to kick off a project, you need to have a team of hardworking and committed individuals. This goes for any recreational project as it does for business. Working with the wrong people is one thing, but *choosing* to work with the wrong people? Yes, it happens. We do it to ourselves sometimes.

The truth is, this stumbling block obstructs you not only if you are in a leadership position, but also if you are a laborer. It is best to work with a team of like-minded individuals, for birds of a feather flock together. But sometimes, you're caught up in the wrong deal. You cannot step out of it. Either you do not recognize it or cannot muster up the strength to leave.

Some signs that you are working with the wrong people are that they bring your character down. Sometimes bringing you physical or financial harm. You may make questionable decisions in their company, feel heavy-hearted, or may even feel limited in your capacity.

If you cannot muster the will to leave, just think about the effects they are having on you and ask yourself, why would you want to work with them now? Why would you put yourself at such a risk?

To give you an example, our former Pastor had a building project where he had people like my husband, who worked in the construction industry for over 20 years. He happened to hire a contractor who took him for his money and did not complete the work. In the end, all of the offerings had gone to this corrupt contractor, about whom, by the way, we tried to warn the Pastor about. The Pastor would not listen. He *chose* to work with this particular contractor. He paid this man despite it all and lost the building.

The Bible talks about Godly counsel. Even our Presidents have a team of Godly counsel. This helps you to stay out of situations that can turn bad for your organization. When there are people that are there to help assist you in listening to them—your spouse more than anyone, I think. Bounce things off them and listen to them. Do not treat them as if their opinion does not matter because, at the end of the day, that person will be there for you. The Bible also states to be in agreement. A husband and wife should always be in agreement. There is power in agreement.

Stumbling Block #6: Not Learning from Previous Mistakes

One scripture that I enjoy studying is about learning from your past and looking into the future.

"18 Forget the former things; do not dwell on the past.

19 See, I am doing a new thing! Now it springs up; do you

not perceive it? I am making a way in the wilderness and streams in the wasteland. **(Isaiah 43:18-19 NIV)**

Dwelling in the past is one thing but keeping the lessons life has taught with you is another. A wise person is someone who learns from the mistakes he or she made in the past. Using that knowledge and lesson, the believer then navigates further.

All people are bound to make mistakes. The Bible states that all have sinned and fallen short of the Glory of God **(Romans 3:23 NIV).** Should that make us falter, or should our mistakes and sins become sources of change for us? Admitting one's mistake and choosing to learn from them is a mature thing. It is another indication of being kind towards yourself.

People stumble when they commit the same mistakes multiple times in their life. You feel trapped if you cannot get out of the hole you keep falling into. It's as simple as looking at the route you are taking and avoiding it the next time. Some people can't seem to exercise this practice. The Bible rightfully includes such people amongst the foolish ones.

"11 As a dog returns to its vomit, so fools repeat their folly.

12 Do you see a person wise in their own eyes? There is more hope for a fool than for them." **(Proverbs 26:11-12 NIV)**

When you are caught in the loop of repeating your mistakes, negativity takes over. Positive traits such as mercy for others and generosity become inaccessible.

The former Pastor was a victim of this stumbling block as well. Remember I narrated earlier about the building he asked us to co-sign? That one lesson apparently was not enough for him. He made another attempt and asked us to co-sign for another building. Not wanting to make the same mistakes again, this time, we did not agree. He went forth with it, found some other people, and they lost that building also. Due to his actions, he has caused others to suffer financially, mentally, emotionally, and spiritually.

On your journey towards generosity and general success in life, you will find certain stumbling blocks that would hinder your progress. Using the example of my former Minister, I gave you six stumbling blocks. Avoiding them on your path will lead you to success. You will become one step closer to the Ministry of Giving and will be able to lead others too.

Chapter 4
Red Flags

In the Scripture, the word 'charity' signifies love, more particularly love for one another. Giving charity is an act of monetary kindness and generosity that requires selflessness and a loving nerve for the other. In Christianity, charity denotes the highest expression of love— equating God and a giver. This was the highest level of giving. He gave the ultimate sacrifice when he gave us his son Jesus. The giver gives out of them self. More so, it also strengthens our relationship with Christ. So, when you're giving to charity, picture yourself helping Christ, because by serving others, you are serving Jesus.

However, the pure connection of giving is contaminated when any negative attitude gets mixed with it. For instance, when we give to be perceived as a virtuous person. About this, the Bible has strictly said:

"2 Thus, when you give to the needy, sound no trumpet before you, as the hypocrites do in the synagogues and in the streets, that others may praise them.

3 Truly, I say to you, they have received their reward.

4 But when you give to the needy, do not let your left hand know what your right hand is doing, so that your giving may be in secret.

5 And your Father who sees in secret, will reward you." (*Matthew 6:2-5 ESV*)

The same happens when another person forces us to give, usually through emotional blackmail or manipulation. This is what I focus on in this chapter. In such a case, your compassion and love for the other person is compromised.

The Bible talks about giving reluctantly or without love at several places. To quote a few:

"Give generously to them and do so without a grudging heart; then because of this, the Lord your God will bless you in all your work and in everything you put your hand to." (*Deuteronomy 15:10 NIV*)

"Every man according as he purposeth in his heart, so let him give; not grudgingly, or of necessity, for God loves a cheerful giver." (*2 Corinthians 9:7 KJV*)

Giving Money Under Pressure

As the above verses show, God loves a cheerful giver, not a pressured giver. Every person has a spirit. Our inner spirit (man) bears witness. The Bible calls this an unction.

"But ye have an unction from the Holy One, and ye know all things." (*1 John 2:20 KJV*)

No matter how we lie to ourselves, our spirit knows the truth.

Giving money is one of the hardest things in a Christian's life. It requires us to truly trust lean, and rely on God to move and ascend in the Ministry of Giving. God has blessed us generously; it is our responsibility, then, to generously pass it onto others. *"Each of you must bring a gift in proportion to the way the Lord your God has blessed you."* (*Deuteronomy 16:17, NIV*)

Building a generous spirit can take time. While you are either developing that love and compassion for others or have already started participating in the Ministry of giving, somebody else can take advantage and manipulate you into giving charity. The action of manipulating someone is one of the wicked things you will encounter in the Ministry of giving. Rather these are priests, ministers, or fellow

Christians, they will pose as if they are guiding you for your own advantage, but this is often done unfairly and dishonestly.

One who forces you to give charity does the following three things: emotionally manipulates and guilt trips you for your money; controls the power to influence or direct your behavior or the course of events, or persuades you that you are out of order for not giving generously to them.

It is crucial to notice such red flags or warnings. My husband and I ignored these signs because we loved our former Pastor so much. But God has put an unction inside of us all, and it's essential not to overlook or override that. The unction or red flags you feel on the inside of you will save you.

Red Flag #1 Don't Practice What You Preach

Someone who does not practice what they preach is a hypocrite. Putting on a show of self-sacrifice for self-glorification is hypocritical and one of the vilest things you can do. The Bible says:

"If anyone thinks he is religious and does not bridle his tongue but deceives his heart, this person's religion is worthless." (*James 1:26, ESV*)

And again:

"Do you suppose, O man—you who judge those who practice such things and yet do them yourself—that you will escape the judgment of God?" (*Romans 2:3, ESV*)

Among charitable people, you may encounter people who urge you to contribute from your wealth for the poor or for some service. When you inspect them, you will see they do not give out of themselves. These ministers or priests usually act as self-righteous individuals. They think God will not detect their lies, but they are wrong. The Bible has clearly mentioned that our hypocrisy doesn't fool God.

" Jesus addressed them directly, 'You always want to look spiritual in the eyes of others,' but you have forgotten the eyes of God, which see what is inside you. The very things that you approve of and applaud are the things which God despises.'" (*Luke 16:15, TPT*)

When my husband and I were in our previous Church, we overlooked certain things. The Pastor would always tell us to reserve some money and save it, but he himself wouldn't do that. He would preach to the people never to go to anyone's party without bringing a gift. Still, he would show up to a party without a gift.

I am glad we ultimately saw the red flags.

Red Flag #2 Ignores or Covers Wrong Doings

Ignorance, as opposed to knowledge, is an inherent human trait. In general, ignorance is not a condemnable trait. The moment it pairs with the ignorance of God's laws or covering it up to save face, that is when innocence ignorance transforms into sin. To quote the Bible:

"My people are destroyed for lack of knowledge; because you have rejected knowledge, I reject you from being a priest to me. And since you have forgotten the law of your God, I also will forget your children." (*Hosea 4:6, ESV*)

As God says in (*Deuteronomy 1:39 ESV*), children have no knowledge of good and evil. But as grown-ups, we have to take a stand against the wrong things going around us. We know from the Bible that God shuts the eyes and hearts of people so that they cannot see or understand. It is when people who are the preachers of the Bible or pose as avid scholars carry on their wicked ways, they become as bad as a non-believer in God's eyes. The Bible says:

"They are darkened in their understanding, alienated from the life of God because of the ignorance that is in them, due to their hardness of heart." (*Ephesians 4:18, ESV*)

Allow me to give you another example of my Old Minister using his wife, who was the Church administrator. I told her about an unjust situation that happened to one of my children when they were 14 years old. She never said anything to me, nor helped in my case, turning a blind eye. It tore me up inside, and I immediately felt the red flag. I ended up speaking with a social worker about the situation. The social worker told me my rights as a mother and tried to get me to press charges. I was told that in the state of Florida, there is no statute of limitations on the issue I had and that if I decide to press charges, the administrator will also go to jail. The social worker took the name of the Church and the administrator down and recorded it.

Red Flag #3 Fraud; Not Using Resources for Intended Purposes.

At its most basic, fraud is the lack of integrity. On integrity, the Bible says:

"Whoever walks in integrity walks securely, but he who makes his ways crooked will be found out." (*Proverbs 10:9, ESV*)

Fraud is equivalent to stealing, lying, and breaking the law all at once. From lying on your tax return to usurping your employee's bonus fee via deception, all count as fraud. All fraud is sinful. I fail to understand how someone can thank God for treasures either brought on or spent by dishonest gain? It doesn't matter how you lie or comfort yourself on the outside; inside, you are well aware of the fraud.

Scams and fraud are brought on by the love of money and the lack of trust in God. Rather than trying to gain quick money through illegal or unethical means, one should aspire to gain little by little. The wealth that is hard-earned with integrity will be spent wisely. Otherwise, it will bring bad fortune and wrath, just as the Bible says:

"Bread gained by deceit is sweet to a man, but afterward, his mouth will be full of gravel." (*Proverbs 20:17, ESV*)

The Pastor and his wife also got grant money to do a summer school program, but they never paid the workers as was promised. Two years passed, and those people still have not gotten paid. This was done two years in a row. The Minister committed fraud.

Red Flag #4 Utilizing Other People's Money as Your Own

I consider utilizing other people's money as your own as the worst kind of selfish act, about which the Bible says:

"3 In whatever you do, don't let selfishness or pride be your guide. Be humble, and honor others more than yourselves.

4 Don't be interested only in your own life, but care about the lives of others too." (*Philippians 2:3-4, ERV*)

Conceiving of other people's money as your own and manipulating them to use their wealth for yourself is a form of bullying. Manipulation meets self-interest here and thrives on the suffering of an innocent person.

The people who may wish bad for you while posing as your friends, only to consume your wealth, will find you gullible and easy to cheat. But I warn you against such deceit. They will use their apparent sophisticated knowledge of the Bible to position themselves as the righteous authority who have the right to do whatever they want with you. They forget that what they think they gain is, in fact, going to bite them later.

"Treasures gained by wickedness do not profit, but righteousness delivers from death." (***Proverbs 10:2, ESV***)

I have narrated several similar incidents of my former Minister regarding this trait. He always looked to others to fulfill his lifestyle. He would pressure the congregation to give and make you feel terrible if you didn't give or did not have anything to contribute. Such people spoil the experience of the Ministry of giving for you. Beware of them.

Red Flag #5 Improper Use of Money

There are many ways you can misuse your money. Uncontrollable spending is one of the ways that can lead to you going into debt and can really impact your family negatively. It can also blind you to spend on things you do not need. According to biblical teachings, this is an indication of greed, which can bring adversity.

Another improper use of money is not spending enough money, i.e., being stingy. When Christians are stingy, they usually never realize it. You can be a philanthropist and still be stingy, for you may not give as much as you can afford to. And then some people give, but with a grudging heart. We must not be lovers of self and lovers of money, which is where stinginess is rooted in. Think about others, just like how Christ thought about us. Give with a cheerful heart without expecting anything in return, for the Bible about a stingy soul says:

"The stingy person hastens after riches and does not know that poverty will overtake him." (**Proverbs 28:22** NIV)

People are worth more than material things, but improper spenders do not know that. Storing up your treasures or spending on luxuries that one does not need is a malicious way to use money. It is always better to help others.

My former Minister would deter from paying the Church's bills and would make the bill collectors would call my husband, who had neither the responsibility of the

Church nor control of the Church's money. The Pastor and his wife handled the money, but they would always look to my husband, myself, and two other couples to pay the Church's bill. The same would be the case when some Church function would take place, or we would rent equipment.

The truth of giving is that it comes from within, and its reward is, in fact, most effective when it comes from within. A generous giver knows the frailty of wealth and money that is given to them and seeks to do good with it. As the Bible says:

"4 Do not wear yourself out to get rich; do not trust your own cleverness.

5 Cast but a glance at riches, and they are gone, for they will surely sprout wings and fly off to the sky like an eagle." (*Proverbs 23:4-5, NIV*)

As hurdles for our generosity, we find people in our lives who exploit the Ministry of giving, berate, critique, attack, belittle, condemn or produce guilt in us when we, for whatever reason, do not help their cause. Their unethical judgmental and accusations spoil our practice of giving because our heart is no longer into it. In this chapter, you saw the five red flags that give you an indication of such manipulators who take advantage of your wealth. They take advantage of you in regard to making you feel spiritually inferior. You should, possible, resist their influence and give only out of the unction that God has placed on the inside of you. You will know when and what to give in the Ministry of giving.

Chapter 5
Integrity

I will define what integrity is and the importance of integrity, considering the Scripture. In the end, we will also study the seven behaviors to keep in mind if you want to become a Christian who has integrity.

Hypocrisy is the opposite of integrity, and this is precisely what Jesus accuses the Pharisees and teachers of the law in *Matthew 23:13, 15, 23, 24, 27, 29 NIV.* There are six times in this sermon that Jesus calls them "*hypocrites.*"

Hypocrisy and the Bible

A hypocrite is a person who pretends to have virtues, moral or religious beliefs, principles, etc., that he or she does not actually possess. This type of person is especially one whose actions belie stated beliefs. In other words, a hypocrite is someone who puts on a mask and pretends to be someone he or she is not. In the Matthew chapter above mentioned, the Bible says:

"13 Woe to you, teachers of the law and Pharisees, you hypocrites!... 14 Woe to you, teachers of the law and Pharisees, you hypocrites! You travel over land and sea to win a single convert, and when he becomes one, you make him twice as much a son of hell as you are. 15 Woe to you, blind guides! You say, `If anyone swears by the temple, it means nothing; but if anyone swears by the gold of the temple, he is bound by his oath.'" **(Matthews 23:13-15 NIV)**

Jesus said this to the Pharisees, who had murderous intentions for him. Their actions went in contrary to their beliefs, so Jesus confronted them.

In our lives, we will come across plenty of hypocrites. A religious figure in the Church or a television evangelist may be teaching you to apply Biblical principles in living a virtuous and godly Christian life; they do not practice what they might be teaching you.

In light of the Ministry of giving, we will encounter people who preach about giving, but they do not give themselves. This happened to my husband and I, as you know. The preacher's attitude, his lack of integrity disheartened us.

I came across others who were narrating things that my husband told me were not the truth. Their sources were unreliable, and my husband's research turned out to be true. So, their words and actions disillusioned me and made me realize how hypocritical people can be. In reality, so many times, they wear masks to hide.

When I discovered the truth, it made me not trust anything that they spoke after that. I do not deny the fact that they trained us Biblically and opened doors of knowledge we did not have access to earlier, in our Christian walk. My life has grown leaps and bounds from beyond that phase.

Hypocrites are not only restricted to the Church. You will find them everywhere. In Matthew chapter 7, the Bible mentions something similar again:

Why do you look at the speck of sawdust in your brother's eye and pay no attention to the plank in your own eye? 4 How can you say to your brother, 'Let me take the speck out of your eye,' when all the time there is a plank in your own eye? 5 You hypocrite, first take the plank out of your own eye, and then you will see clearly to remove the speck from your brother's eye." (**Matthew 7:3-5 NIV**)

Note that the word "*plank*" in Greek means a large load-bearing beam. But what the parable above mean? It simply states if anyone, Pastor, or preacher ever hopes to "criticize" or express his or her opinion thoughtfully to another person, they should first assure their own sight is uninhibited. This, of course, goes across all fields of practice and discipline.

What is Integrity?

Integrity is the exercise of being truthful and authentic in all things that you do. A person who has integrity displays consistent and unyielding adherence to strong moral and ethical principles and values. The question of integrity is not only a focus point in Christianity and Bible studies but also in the field of ethics and philosophy. Integrity tends to stand in contrast to hypocrisy. As opposed to wearing masks and showing contradicting behaviors, integrity is the alignment with the truth within and being honest.

The standards of integrity involve internal consistency as a key virtue. It suggests that Christians holding conflicting values within themselves should first come to terms and acknowledge the discrepancy in their own actions. If we consider the etymology of the word integrity, it evolved from the Latin adjective 'integer,' meaning whole or complete. We also use the term 'integer' for numbers that are whole and cannot be broken down into fractional components, for example, 21 or 2048. This mathematical concept brings insight to the trait of integrity, that a person's 'wholeness' is maintained intact. None of their actions can be broken down into anything that is not authentic.

So, we observe that integrity is the inner sense of "wholeness" deriving from qualities such as honesty and consistency of character. As such, one may judge that others "have integrity" to the extent that they act according to the values, beliefs, and principles they claim to hold. A significant aspect of integrity is that a Christian who has integrity is honest, even about their dishonesty.

Integrity and the Bible

Let us look at the various ways in which the Bible preaches to us about integrity.

"5 Better is open rebuke than hidden love. 6 The wounds of a friend are faithful, but the kisses of an enemy are deceitful." (Proverbs 27:5-6 NIV)

Another verse in the same chapter goes:

"Whoever rebukes a person will, in the end, gain favor rather than one who has a flattering tongue." **(Proverbs 28:23 NIV)**

The pattern here is that with integrity, you get straightforward authenticity. If you do not like someone's food, you tell the person you don't like it, as kindly as possible, of course. If you wrongfully assure them that the food they cook is great, they may be deceived, and it will hurt more when hearing the truth form other people. In the end, integrity in all things rewards you in the best way. It is about confronting your problems when it would be easier to walk away.

Integrity is also about keeping a promise when you would rather not. Whether it be due to circumstances or things coming up at the last second, you must try your best to fulfill a promise made. It establishes that you have honor and that you are generous. Indeed, making a promise and delivering on it is a sign of giving and generosity. The Bible talks about it in Psalm, where God answers the question of who will dwell on His holy mountain.

"Who despises a vile person but honors those who fear the Lord; who keeps an oath even when it hurts, and does

not change their mind;" (*Psalm 15 NIV*)

Integrity is one of the essential parts of all our relationships. Employers expect integrity in their employees, for they must be able to trust them and depend upon them. Husbands expect their wives to have integrity, and wives expect the same of their husbands. When a person lies and cheats, or acts two-face, they cause other people not to trust them.

We Christians have the model of the life of Jesus as a life symbolic of integrity. He taught the highest of principles and then lived His life embodying those principles. He was the same for everyone. He was the same on every occasion. He was openly honest. He hid nothing and never had a reason to be ashamed because he maintained his contract of integrity between and among all things. His life was such a contrast with the Pharisees that their hatred and jealousy ultimately brought about His death.

As opposed to the teachings of Jesus. It damages our witness, our reputation, and could cause people to disregard even the authentic actions we show, as well as the Gospel message that we should be exemplifying.

How to Maintain Your Integrity?

You read the question right because maintaining integrity can be difficult. So how do you do that?

I mentioned that integrity is fundamental to relationships, but there's more to that. When you sign a contract, you are making a promise of integrity. When you use a credit card, you are making a promise of integrity. When you sign up to do something, when you commit to joining something, when you set an appointment with a doctor or a friend or a professor, when you say you are going to teach a class, when you say you will be there in time for the meeting, basically when you give your word to commit to anything, you are making a promise of integrity. And like I told you, the person with integrity keeps their promises even when he or she would rather not.

There may indeed come times in your life when you stop and think about lying, or deceiving, or doing something that goes against what you stand for. Sometimes, it comes at the end of a chapter of your life. Sometimes, it comes after a crisis in your life. In a nutshell, sometimes your back is up against the wall, which is bound to happen at some point in time, and that is when you choose the easy way out, which is does not exhibit integrity.

Consider the scenario between the cheating husband I mentioned above. Do you think it would be easy for the husband to admit his flaws to his wife? In the short-term, that may be a tempting option, but the truth is, the husband will suffer in the long term, and somewhere inside, his integrity tells him that he is wrong in betraying his wife. I have devised a list of seven behaviors that will preserve your long-term satisfaction and happiness. Be it in your relationships, with people, or things; you should always remember to do the following:

• Tell the truth, because your word is your bond. If there is a change in what you promised someone, especially when it comes to matters involving money, communicate the change openly and sincerely. Let us say you promised a family to give them money, but you found out that you have to reserve the money for something else urgently. Never just keep going on as if nothing happened and shrug off a promise. Instead, tell them your story, work around it another way and hope they will empathize. Not communicating truthfully with people is rude and mean, which will make you less desirable. Integrity has the courage to face the truth and does the right thing because it is right.

- Communicate honestly, which is an important component of integrity. It will always keep the airways clear of confusion. The Bible relates confusion with the evil work of the devil. So be wary.

- Take your commitments and contracts seriously. Once you utter something, people remember it, especially when it is about something that favors them. You cannot simply go selfish and break your contract, especially when you gave the person hope. If your words and actions are not matching up, you will be labeled a hypocrite, but do remember that it is fixable.

- Be responsible. As a leader, you must take ownership when things go wrong, just like you take credit when your team or staff or group or people succeeds – the possibilities are endless. Don't blame others for *your* bad decision-making skills, especially when dealing with a lot of money at stake. Be accountable

- Never put on a false front, ever. Remember that Integrity does not wear a mask. Therefore, say only what you mean to say, nothing else. Integrity means that a person is honest about their beliefs. There is no lying, stealing, cheating, or any deception involved. When making a commitment is not possible, integrity has the courage to say, "*no.*"

- Try to maintain your trust in people, even if you must sacrifice something for yourself. Integrity describes a person who is worthy of complete trust. Without keeping up trust, which comes from the combination of all the above, you can never be a person of integrity.

A lesson in integrity is not just important for the Ministry of giving, but the whole of life. It is easy to be a hypocrite and deceive people, but it is the evil way that means you walk a lonely and undesirable path. On the other hand, integrity may take time to build up and will require you to build patience for long-term gratification.

I hope the teaching in this chapter above, including the six behaviors, in the end, will help you to walk in integrity. People will noticeably see that change in you. Let God have his perfect work in you, and your integrity in the kingdom will be exceptional.

Chapter 6
Purity of Heart

After our discussion on the fundamentals of integrity, it is important to talk about the purity of hearts. There are various indicators of the heart's purity. There is a pure intention for doing good things, such as giving. It is also showing love to all kinds of people. I believe one of the most beautiful expressions of your heart being pure is the virtue of forgiveness.

It is still easy for us to observe a hungry person who is in need and give them money. It is still easy to show love to children for their innocence and to elders for the respect they command. But to look in the eye at someone who wronged you, who became a cause of your suffering, and to say those golden words, "I forgive you," it doesn't get any purer than that.

In this chapter, we will talk about forgiveness and the reasons why we should forgive others. It might surprise you, but forgiving others correlates with the work you do in the Ministry of giving. It can help us exalt to a place that is nearer to God. Therefore, when our Father, who is in Heaven, watches you be gentle and forgiving towards those of his children that are wrongdoers, He trusts you to be a distribution center with the money that he places in your hand.

The Human Psyche and Forgiveness

Sometimes in our lives, things happen that affect us in a good or bad way. We store those memories and emotions deep inside us, even if at that moment, they may affect us on the surface too. The more terrible and serious events or actions by others tend to impose a long-term impact on us. Sometimes it can be lifelong.

The truth is, we are flawed people. Rather we are bound to make mistakes and hurt each other, whether on purpose or not. The Bible says:

"For all have sinned and fall short of the glory of God." (**Romans 3:23 NIV**)

We are All in Need of Forgiveness

From a spiritual perspective, we were all born not only as sinners but with the inclination to sin through life. If you think about it, the very inception of our life on Earth, following the banishment of Adam from Eden, began from sin. Having separated from God, we were eternally separated from purity. But the purpose of life is to find our way back to God. We will be lost forever without His guidance, and especially as sinners if he does not forgive us.

I often think about my own mistakes, the people I have hurt, and the wrong things I have done, but God has kept my honor and grace. God is there with open arms to offer forgiveness and lift the weight off my chest when I raise my hands in prayer.

When we consider the mercy that God has descended on us, and accept ourselves as flawed people, it gets significantly easier to forgive others for their wrongdoings. They are just people like us, and their wrongs have given us the opportunity to imitate the trait of God.

Along the same lines but considerably different, consider the following verse.

"14 For if you forgive others their trespasses, your heavenly Father will also forgive you, 15 but if you do not forgive others their trespasses, neither will your Father

*forgive your trespasses." (**Matthew 6: 14-15 NIV**)*

This verse is not that difficult to grasp. Knowing that we are flawed people who look up to God for our forgiveness, He who always stands ready and willing to forgive us, those who have wronged us also are looking up to us for forgiveness. God asks that we extend the same mercy towards them and forgive their deviances.

An inability to do so means we may be stone-hearted, and why should God forgive your wrongdoings when you do not forgive someone else's? God hates holding resentment and bitterness in our hearts. Such grudges can make Him punish us for our unforgiveness by blocking our blessings. I know that forgiving someone for a serious offense can be very difficult, but the Bible tells us to forgive one another, so we must build up our tolerance.

It's time to give it over to God by not only showing mercy to others but ourselves too. Indeed, grudges contain negative energy and corrupt the good in our hearts. By building on our ability to forgive, we are practicing mercy towards other people and ourselves alike. If we are empathetic, we see the person who did us wrong in a positive light. Whether they demand forgiveness by themselves or not, we will want to forgive them. It is an expression of kindness and divinity to forgive, as the Bible says:

*"Be kind to one another, tenderhearted, forgiving one another, as God in Christ forgave you." (**Ephesians 4:32 ESV**)*

We can only manage this tenderhearted kindness if we learn to practice forgiveness every day until it becomes a lifestyle. Jesus knew that we have it in us to master forgiveness, which is why this dialogue took place between Christ and Peter.

*"21 Then Peter came up and said to him, "Lord, how often will my brother sin against me, and I forgive him? As many as seven times?" 22 Jesus said to him, "I do not say to you seven times, but seventy times seven." (**Matthew 18:21-22 ESV**)*

Reasons to Build a Forgiving Nature

Jesus indeed calls us to examine our own lives first instead of focusing on the actions of another. If we truly love him, we will follow his example. As we have understood, it can be easier to forgive others when we understand our own shortcomings. But what shortcomings did Jesus have, and yet he forgave the Pharisee woman, saying

*"Neither do I condemn thee: go, and sin no more." (**John 8:11 KJV**)*

Our challenge is to follow Jesus's example and do the same. You must keep in mind that when a person decides not to forgive, it causes bitterness, resentment, and hate to grow. It then becomes very valuable to learn to forgive people when they hurt you; otherwise, your unforgiveness would lead to you having health issues in your body. It can cause you to have blood pressure issues, break your immune system down, cause more stress and anxiety, and that is still just scratching the surface. You can imagine what the inability to forgive could do to you spiritually and psychologically.

On the other hand, when you practice forgiveness, it makes you happier, removes pain and grudges from your heart, kills bitterness and resentment, and the physical ailments they bred in you. Forgiveness frees you in the truest sense and breaks shackles from your thoughts.

My family had suffered a great deal because of certain people, not the least of which was the formet Pastor. I think my husband and I were more bothered than anyone because we could not figure out how someone that says they love you could do such a thing. We could not figure out how to forgive a person so cruel. That is when we turned to God.

Seeking God's Help in Forgiveness

"And whenever you stand praying, forgive, if you have anything against anyone, so that your Father also who is in heaven may forgive you your trespasses." **(Mark 11:25 ESV)**

Showing love to people who hurt you can be difficult, but not with God's help. You have to trust, rely, & lean on the Spirit of God, and He will always bring you through.

If you are someone who finds it difficult to forgive your wrongdoers despite realizing all the above facts, then only the love given to us by the Holy Spirit can transform your heart.

"And hope does not put us to shame, because God's love has been poured into our hearts through the Holy Spirit who has been given to us." **(Romans 5:5, ESV)**

This kind of forgiveness is a Grace, and God does bless it. You may have to ask the Holy Spirit to help you as I did continually day in and out. I would ask Jesus to uncover and unburden my mind and intellect, will and reasoning, emotions, feelings, memory, thoughts, and imagination. I would cry and plead for help. I would ask him, "I need your help. I can't do this on my own." I did not like having a hard heart who could not forgive a trespasser. Thankfully, the Holy Spirit helped my husband and me. Our hearts opened, and prayers were answered. Guess what, we are not in that place any longer. We are Victors, not victims. Jesus said:

*"Whoever claims to love God yet hates a brother or sister is a liar. For whoever does not love their brother and sister, whom they have seen, cannot love God, whom they have not seen." (**1 John 4:20, NIV**)*

The scripture states that if you know what the right thing to do is and you don't do it, then you are committing a sin (***James 4:17KJV***) We do not want to be at that place, not with something so physically and spiritually rewarding as forgiveness.

Forgiveness grants us abundance. It is such a joy to be able to help others. I know what it is like to be with out and have very little; I've been there. When I tell you that forgiveness and abundance are related, I am speaking from experience. I know what it is like to be in abundance and to be able to help someone in need. Therefore, it's better to forgive than to hold on to unforgiveness.

We have seen that forgiveness involves the intentional letting go of grievous acts and sins of others. God throws our sins in the sea of forgetfulness once we repent. Just as God forgives us, we must forgive others. This sometimes can be very hard. However, for the love of Christ, of God, and ourselves, we need to practice forgiveness and make it a part of our lifestyle. We can do so by practicing forgiving daily. When I say lifestyle, I mean, this becomes natural to us to let go and leave it to God and never bring it back up.

Chapter 7
A New Beginning

After improving on and enhancing each of the qualities mentioned in this book, you are now ready for a new beginning. But there are certain requirements that you need to fulfill to become a new person, love for God and Jesus Christ. In this chapter in the end, I will share my experience and transition into being a new person.

The Need for Love of God for a New Beginning

"And we know that all things work together for good to them that love God, to them who are the called according to his purpose." (**Romans 8:28 KJV**)

This verse holds the essence of a Christian, which is the absolute faith in God. If he wants to conduct our lives without falling into the same state of mind that sinners and some saints, for instance, we must have love for God and live to please Him. We, too, are subject to our own unstable convictions, opinions, and decisions. You and I know that God really loves us. It is when we love Him back that the miracles start happening. Things come to work in our favor.

Even when hardships come, we are not angry with God because God did not do anything to us. We become subject to the mistreatment of others, over which we barely have any control. Life may seem unfair during such circumstances, but when we love God and understand how he works, we understand that the trial that has met us is something beneficial for us. If we see through it, things will work in our favor. We will end up better than we started out.

(If you fall to pieces in a crisis, there wasn't much to you in the first place. Proverbs 24:10 MSG)

As Christians, it is so important to develop this perspective and hold on to it resiliently. We must desire and respond to God's grace, His gift of Christ, to His gift of the Holy Ghost, to His blessing of revealing to us knowledge and understanding of what is happening. This responsiveness indeed is what loving God is about.

God calls many towards him, but only a few become part of the elected ones. I am happy to say I feel like one of God's own. I believe I have met the condition of loving God and desiring all that he wants me to desire and chase. God has comforted me in all my difficult times with his assurances in the Bible, touching my heart. Just like He got me out of that old Ministry, he will help you to escape and head towards a new beginning. Now I am really aware of how a ministry should operate. The new Ministry is all about love, unity, and freedom, and I wouldn't trade it for anything.

(Behold how good and how pleasant it is for brethren to dwell together in unity Psalms 133:1 KJV)

God loves when brethren dwell together in unity. This is where God will command the blessings. I love how the Man and Women of God work together; they flow with harmony. The people are so genuine in this new Ministry. When I first came here, I was amazed at how well a Man and Women of God flow together in unity in Ministry.

We visit another ministry every year in July, the week of my birthday, and this is how the other Ministry operates as well. They are in another state, but they fill me up with so much love, and they are so genuine. My impression had been contaminated because of the old Ministry and the former Pastor, but I found the new Ministry is all about wanting God to heal us. They do not try to pimp us for money. It is the embodiment of the Romans verse above, operating in the love of God and aligned with his purpose.

The Need for Love of Christ for a New Beginning

"Therefore, if anyone is in Christ, he is a new creation. The old has passed away; behold, the new has come." (2 Corinthians 5:17 ESV)

"Now thanks be unto God, which always causeth us to triumph in Christ, and maketh manifest the savior of his knowledge by us in every place." (Corinthians 2:14 KJV)

Christ loves all of us. We are embraced unto him, special, and preserved in his heart. When a person believes in Christ and gives themselves up to him, Christ brings a beautiful transformation into his or her life. The person evolves and is in the process of becoming a new creature.

Changes begin to take place internally. All the contaminants of the soul erode, and space is made for new, beautiful characteristics and thoughts. An inward principle of grace develops, and the new man or woman is a completely different person from the old. The corruption of their nature is gone, and something new has been planted in the soul, which never was there before. Love of Christ improves the old principles of nature, and our souls meet grace and holiness. We are the recipients of a new heart and a new spirit.

In them, we embrace new light and life, new affections and desires, new delights and joys. Our vision is renewed, our capacity to hear, touch, walk, and work, all experience a revival. You no longer want to be with the old companions and acquaintances. External things such as riches, honors, knowledge, former religious beliefs, all undergo a beautiful transformation.

"Behold, I am doing a new thing; now it springs forth, do you not perceive it? I will make a way in the wilderness and rivers in the desert." **(Isaiah 43:19 ESV)**

A new trajectory and experience of life open up for you. Christ awakens and amplifies our faith and bliss. We learn about a new way of serving God through Christ. This is what the Bible meant by the passing away of old ways and all things becoming new.

God makes a way in the wilderness of our hearts and rivers in our minds so that thoughts flow freely. I have been blessed to undergo these changes and feel covered in the glory of the Lord and Jesus Christ as a new creation in him.

My New Beginning

"22 To put off your old self, which belongs to your former manner of life and is corrupt through deceitful desires,

23 and to be renewed in the spirit of your minds,

24 and to put on the new self, created after the likeness of God in true righteousness and holiness." **(Ephesians 4:22-24 ESV)**

I am so thankful for the Ministry I am part of now and two other Ministries that have been praying for us. It has been a true experience for both my husband and I as we interacted with the true devotees of God and love. If it weren't for these ministries, we wouldn't have stepped foot in any other church, but glory be unto God, who always leads us to triumph.

This is our new beginning. I am so happy to embark on this journey. My Father has truly transformed me from inside out. I never thought that I could truly be this happy in a ministry. It is true that when God sets you free, you are free, indeed. No more bondage, no more grief, no more pain. I feel today like how I felt when I first accepted Jesus into my life 23 years ago.

I can say that I have money. I am truly happy in my life. For the first time in a long time, I am happy in Jesus. This is our new beginning.

As for my old journey, I have let that go. I knew that I could not harbor anything negative in my heart if I truly desire God's grace. You must ask God to help you in forgiving those who did wrong by you in the past too. It may take you some time, but as we saw in the last chapter, too, forgiveness is a fundamental step. There is no new beginning with old grudges.

The former Pastor hurt my whole family because of his lust for money. Some of my family members still have trust issues because of him. The joy I feel today after forgiving him is better than the bitterness that I held in my heart.

Even after following all the guidelines in this book, you have to love God and Jesus Christ to begin a brand new journey. In this chapter, you learned what love for God and Christ entails, and how it can change us. I gave you a glimpse of my experience and how I transitioned from struggling to becoming happy.

On the parting note, this will be my advice to you: If you are unhappy in life, reevaluate what it is that disturbs you about your experience, and make the necessary change, be it of the Church or Pastor, or any other thing. You will acquire clarity and will feel much happier.

Before we part, I would like to add this prayer below.

Prayer for Salvation and Baptism of the Holy Spirit

Heavenly Father, I come to you in the name of Jesus. Your Word says,

"Whosoever shall call on the name of the Lord shall be saved." (*Acts 2:21 KJV*)

I am calling on you. I pray, and I ask Jesus to come into my heart and be my Lord, as the scripture states,

"If thou shall confess with thou mouth the Lord Jesus, and shall believe in thine heart that God raised Jesus from the dead, thou shall be saved. For with the heart that man believeth unto righteousness; and with the mouth, confession is made unto salvation." (*Romans 10:9-10 KJV*)

I do that now. I confess that Jesus is Lord, and I believe in my heart that God raised Jesus from the dead.

I am now reborn! I am a Christian, a child of Almighty God! I am saved! You also said in your Word:

"If ye then, being evil, know how to give good gifts unto your children: HOW MUCH MORE shall your heavenly Father give the Holy Spirit to them that ask him?" **(Luke 11:13 KJV)**

I'm also asking you to fill me up with the Holy Spirit. Holy Spirit rises up within me as I praise God. I fully expect to speak with other tongues as you give me utterance **(Acts 2:4 KJV)**. In Jesus' name, Amen!

I will ask you to begin to praise God for filling you with the Holy Spirit. Speak those words and syllables you receive not in your own language, but the language was given to you by the Holy Spirit. You have to use your own voice, though. God will not force you to speak. Don't be concerned with how it sounds. It's a heavenly language!

Continue with the blessing God has given you and pray in the spirit every day. You are born again, Spirit-filled believer. You will never be the same! Find a good church that preaches God's Word and obeys it. Become a part of a church family who will love you and care for you as you love and care for them. We need to be connected to each other. It increases our strength in God. It is God's plan for us.

Become a doer of the word, who is blessed in his doing (*James 1:22-25 KJV*).

HOW TO PROPERLY RELATE IN THE MINISTRY OF GIVING